08/10
9.95

It!

It!

It!

SMASH It! CRASH It! LAUNCH It!

50 Mind-BLOWING EYE-Popping Science Experiments

Rain Newcomb & Bobby Mercer

LARK BOOKS

A Division of
Sterling Publishing Co., Inc.
New York / London

Editor:
VERONIKA ALICE GUNTER

Creative Director:
CELIA NARANJO

Art Production Assistant:
BRADLEY NORRIS

Editorial Assistance:
DAWN DILLINGHAM,
DELORES GOSNELL, AND
ROSE McLARNEY

The Library of Congress has cataloged the hardcover edition as follows:

Newcomb, Rain.
  Smash it! crash it! launch it! : 50 mind-blowing, eye-popping science
experiments / by Rain Newcomb and Bobby Mercer ; illustrated by Tom
LaBaff.
      p. cm.
  Includes index.
  ISBN-13: 978-1-57990-795-2
  ISBN-10: 1-57990-795-4
  1. Science--Experiments--Juvenile literature. I. Mercer, Bobby, 1961- II.
LaBaff, Tom, ill. III. Title.
  Q164.N475 2006
  507.8--dc22
                                        2006005518

10 9 8 7 6 5 4 3 2 1

Published by Lark Books, A Division of
Sterling Publishing Co., Inc.
387 Park Avenue South, New York, N.Y. 10016

First Paperback Edition 2009
Text © 2006, Lark Books
Illustrations © 2006, Tom LaBaff

Distributed in Canada by Sterling Publishing,
c/o Canadian Manda Group, 165 Dufferin Street
Toronto, Ontario, Canada M6K 3H6

Distributed in the United Kingdom by GMC Distribution Services,
Castle Place, 166 High Street, Lewes, East Sussex, England BN7 1XU

Distributed in Australia by Capricorn Link (Australia) Pty Ltd.,
P.O. Box 704, Windsor, NSW 2756 Australia

If you have questions or comments about this book, please contact:
Lark Books
67 Broadway
Asheville, NC 28801
(828) 253-0467

Manufactured in China

ISBN 13: 978-1-57990-795-2 (hardcover) 978-60059-509-7 (paperback)

For information about custom editions, special sales, premium and corporate purchases, please
contact Sterling Special Sales Department at 800-805-5489 or specialsales@sterlingpub.com.

Contents

It Is Rocket Science

Rocket scientists have the most fun. I know because my Mom's a rocket scientist. She's encouraged me to build catapults, bottle rockets, and boomerangs since I could hold a bottle of glue. Sometimes she even lets me come to the office with her. Only occasionally has she said, "Jessie, I don't think *that's* an appropriate item for launching." Usually she's talking about one of my brother's toys, or a file on her desk marked "Top Secret."

Recently, I've begun an in-depth study of **destructology** with the help of my friends Lucinda and Tim. (Destructology is our study of how different items—mostly fruits and vegetables—explode when they hit the ground). Mom supports this research, too. She says it's all part of having a "well-rounded scientific foundation." Which sounds like a good thing to me.

Now that we've had so much fun, Lucinda, Tim, and I want to share some of our favorite experiments with you. We've collected more than 50 activities that are guaranteed to thrill you and your friends. You'll make everyday objects soar, crash, or smash—and sometimes do all three.

How amazingly cool are these projects? First of all, a lot of the activities make a mess. Have you ever flipped a bucket full of water upside down over your head? You won't get wet—as long as **Newton's First** and **Third**
Laws of Motion** are on your side. (See page 32.) And how about harnessing the power of candy to empty a soda bottle at lightning speed? That's one of my favorite equations: **Pressure** plus **momentum** equals soda everywhere. (See page 60.) Don't worry—if you follow our instructions, the messes are only as big as you want them to be and won't provoke a freak-out by your parental units.

So what does science have to do with all this fun? Everything! All the activities in this book work because of science, from the rules governing **vertical forces** to **Bernoulli's Principles** about fluids to chemistry, and more. You'll read about the science in the "What's Going On?" section that follows each set of instructions.

Some of these activities are so much fun you'll want to do them over and over again. Once you've built a mini-marshmallow catapult, how about building a catapult large enough to launch your stinky gym shoes into your washing machine so you don't have to touch them? The science is the same. Once you understand the science, well, you can do anything.

Rocket science sounds hard, but I think it's because of the math used to prove the theories on paper. The theories themselves aren't hard to understand. So, I say save the math for school, and let's have fun. Who has time for long division when there are tomatoes to splat?

Ready to Make Some Explosive Discoveries?

Destructology sounds like a field of study that could get you in trouble. But these are law-abiding experiments. Really. They follow laws like Newton's Laws of Motion. All of the experiments in this book can be explained using mathematical equations—but you don't need to know any math to enjoy this book.

Outside of the labs where Lucinda, Tim, and I work, destructology is a subset of the study of physics. Physics is the science of **matter**, **energy**, and their interactions. It applies to any matter and the forces that act on it. So, physics applies to everything around you. If you let go of this book, it falls to the ground because **force** (**gravity**) acts upon matter (the book). If you throw this book, you are the force acting on the matter, propelling it forward. If your friend throws it back, hits you,

and it makes you stagger, you're the matter, and the force acting on you is the energy of your friend's throw. All of this is physics in action.

But, don't throw this book anywhere yet. Physics will make a lot more sense—and get a lot more interesting—as you use this book. When you're knocking over stacks of nickels, crushing cans with bricks, and watching grapes spark in the microwave, you'll be experimenting with momentum, **inertia**, force, and energy.

After you conduct the experiments, you'll be able to understand how surfboards, hang gliders, and hot-air balloons work. And you'll be prepared to make new and improved straw launchers, balloon dragsters, potato poppers, and other significant scientific contraptions.

How to Use This Book

Read the instructions carefully all the way through, gather your materials, and you're ready to have a smashing good time. You can do a lot of these experiments on your own. We'll tell you when to have an adult lend a hand.

To get started, you don't have to know a lot about science. But, if you read the "What's Going On?" explanation after each set of instructions, you'll be a science whiz by the time you're through with this book. It also helps to look up words you don't know. Words and phrases in **bold** are defined in the glossary on page 76 of this book.

Be prepared to do the experiments more than once. Trying out different ways of doing things is what experimenting is all about. (And who wouldn't want a reason to crush another egg?)

Lab (and Launch Pad) Rules

This *is* rocket science, after all, so there are some special guidelines you'll want to follow.

Ask an adult for permission to conduct the experiments and make sure that the place you

choose for your lab is okay with them. If you can, it's fun to do a lot of these experiments outside. But, don't conduct them in the middle of the flower bed. Likewise, when instructions tell you to set up your karate chop experiment on a table, it might be best to choose the worktable in the garage instead of the dining room table.

Copy this list of guidelines and hang it up when you're experimenting so that you'll always know what to do.

- **Read through each experiment before starting.**
- **Collect all your materials. You may need an adult to help you find or buy some of them at a grocery or drug store.**
- **Wear protective gear whenever the instructions specify.**
- **Aim the rockets, balls, and other scientific devices away from people, animals, your siblings, etc. (Don't aim them at windows or other breakable things either.)**
- **After using raw eggs in an experiment, wash your hands well.**
- **Always ask an adult to help you if the activity instructions say you should, if you aren't sure what to do, or if you have questions.**
- **Clean up after you finish your experiments.**

Now, put on your lab coat and your goggles (or your bathing suit and your goggles, as the case might be). You're ready to *Smash It! Crash It! Launch It!*

Splat!

Toss veggies out the window so that they'll explode on the driveway. Do it for science.

What You Need

- Proper location (see step 1)
- Old tomatoes and melons
- Tennis ball or bouncy ball
- Good clean-up skills

What You Do

1. Find a safe location and get a parent's permission to do this experiment. You can use a deck or a window to provide the needed elevation. A driveway is the best surface to land the objects on, but it's not required.

2. Drop the tomato. What happens? Drop the bouncy ball. What was different?

3. Drop other things and see what happens.

4. Clean up. Science is a messy business.

What's Going On?

Collisions are an integral part of our everyday life. They can be amazing (the kind you see in an action movie), or they can be almost unnoticeable (your foot hitting the ground as you walk).

Energy and **momentum** must be **conserved** in all collisions, according to the **Law of Conservation of Momentum** and the **Law of Conservation of Energy**. (That means the energy can't just disappear.) The energy and momentum are what explode the tomato you drop.

Collisions primarily involve **thermal** and **kinetic energy**. Clap your hands together. They heat up—create thermal energy—because of the collision. Old tomatoes go splat; that is, they have an **inelastic collision**, which means they lose all of their kinetic energy. Where did it go? Most of the energy was turned into heat; a little bit of it went into making the SPLAT noise; and some it went into the ground. Both the ground and the squashed tomato will be warmer because of the collision. (You can try the experiment again and see if you can feel the difference in temperature.)

The ball only loses part of its kinetic energy and bounces back up instead of splatting. In a perfectly **elastic collision**, the ball would bounce back to the original height, because its energy transformed from potential to kinetic energy and back again without losing anything.

Tomato Tower

Build a gravity-defying tower with a few sheets of newspaper, and then test its strength with a tomato. Only the tomato will be harmed.

What You Need

- Easy-to-clean, flat location
- At least 5 sheets of newspaper
- Tape
- Scissors
- Old tomatoes

What You Do

1. Roll each sheet of newspaper from one long end to the other to make five newspaper "straws." Tape around the end of each newspaper straw to hold it together.

2. Stand one of the straws up on the floor. You will need to flare the base of the straw (making it wider than the top) so it can stand on its own.

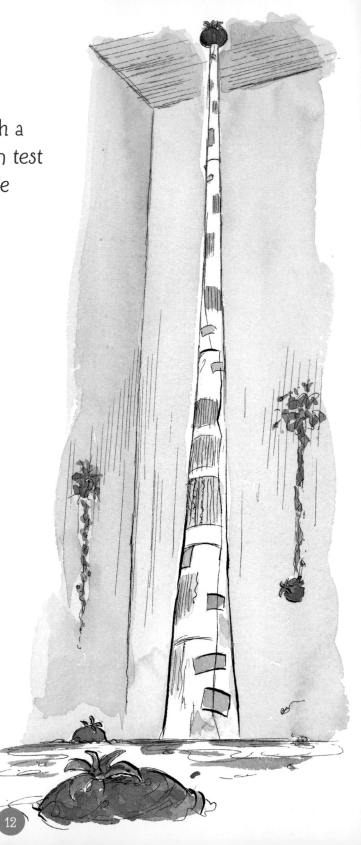

3. Add the next newspaper straw to your tower by inserting one end into the standing straw. Put the tomato on the tower. Does it balance on top, or does it fall and splat? If it stands, remove the tomato and add another straw to the tower. As you add each straw, make any minor adjustments you need so that the tower continues to stand. The bottom straw will have to be the widest. Then place the tomato on top again.

4. Keep adding straws and testing the tower with the tomato. See how high you can go.

5. Build the tower again using five sheets of newspaper rolled any way you like. You can even use scissors to cut the newspaper into smaller pieces. Experiment with cutting the paper into triangle-shapes before rolling them into straws. Did you get a taller tower? A stronger tower? Ketchup?

6. Challenge your friends to top your tower.

What's Going On?

People have been trying to build structures taller than themselves since the Stone Age. Towers are the tallest structures built. Look at towers where you live, in books, or on the Internet. What do you see? The first thing you'll notice is that they're not made out of newspaper. The next thing you'll probably notice is that most towers—cellular phone towers, radio towers, the Eiffel Tower—resemble a stack of triangles.

That's because the triangle is the strongest shape for holding **weight** and handling **forces**. (Weight is caused by the pull of the Earth's **gravity**.) The weight includes the weight of the materials plus whatever is in the tower. (In your tower, the weight is the newspaper and the tomato.) All this weight is **vertical force** pulling down on the base of the tower. The tower is also affected by **horizontal forces**, namely, the wind blowing at it from the sides.

Your tower is a very skinny modified triangle. In your tower, the weight of the tomato and all the sheets of newspaper are all bearing down on the tower's base. Flaring out the base makes it act like a triangle. A triangle distributes the vertical force along an angle which redirects part of the force in a horizontal direction. That's what made it possible for your tower to support the tomato.

Karate Chop

Use the strength of air to break a board with your hand.

What You Need

- Thin strip of wood, less than ¼ inch thick
- Table
- Full sheet of newspaper

What You Do

1. Place the strip of wood on a table with half of the strip hanging over the edge.

2. Karate chop the strip of wood. Does anything happen?

3. Smooth out the sheet of newspaper and place it over the strip. The newspaper should extend all the way to the edge of the table, but not off the table (see illustration). Press the newspaper down to squish out all the air.

4. Give the strip your best downward karate chop. (Give your best karate chop yell as well.) What happens?

What's Going On?

Have you ever noticed when you swim in a pool that you feel the water pressing on your body? Air presses on your body all the time like that, but you don't often feel it. You might take air for granted, since it's always there.

As you swim deeper in the pool, the **force** of the water pressing on your body will grow. The added force is because you have more water pressing down on you.

Pressure is the amount of force pressing on an **area** of your body. **Air pressure** is the force from air pressing onto your body. It's like your body is in a 3,280,840-foot deep pool of air. Air pressure at sea level is almost 15 pounds acting on each square inch of your skin. Your body is used to this feeling, so you don't notice it.

So what's that have to do with your karate chop? Everything. You get rid of the air under the newspaper when you squish it out. Now, you only have air pressure on the top of the paper. Since the paper is big, the force exerted by air is big. Your chop's force will be less than the force of air holding the paper down, so the board breaks. If you just push on the board slowly, air rushes under the paper, and the air pressure on both sides of the newspaper would be equal and the board would not break.

Banana Split

That's what you get when you fling a banana at your mom.

What You Need

- Adult helper
- Sharp knife
- Bananas (perfect use for disgusting brown bananas)

What You Do

1. Have your adult helper hold the knife at arm's length, pointing up with the blade facing you. Tell your helper that she absolutely cannot move during the experiment. Then tell her you'll be throwing bananas at her.

2. Peel the banana. Stand 5 or 6 feet away from your helper. Throw the banana, aiming for the knife. If you miss, try again. What happens when you hit the knife? (What happens if you hit your helper?)

3. After you've successfully sliced the banana on the knife a few times, take a step back and start throwing the banana pieces at the knife. What happens?

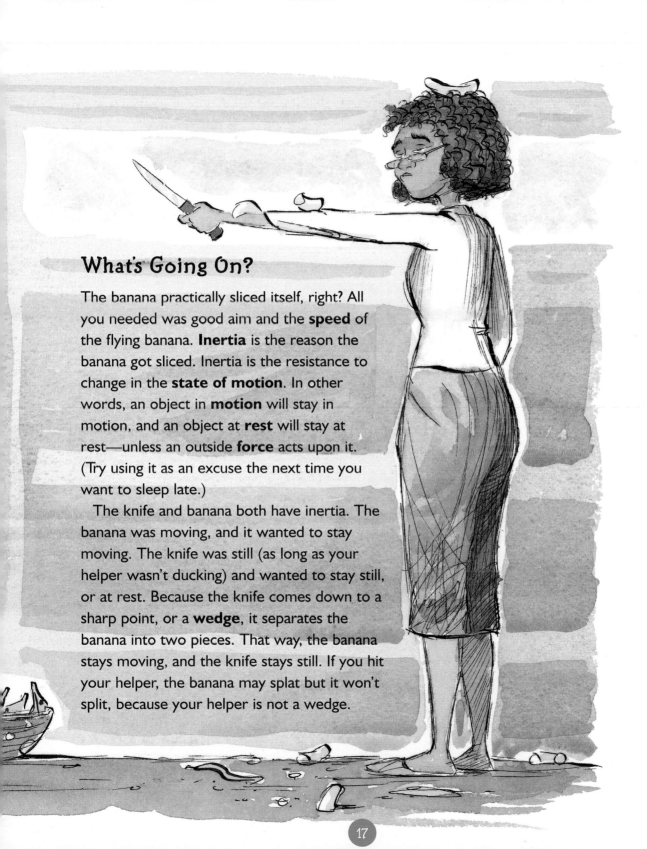

What's Going On?

The banana practically sliced itself, right? All you needed was good aim and the **speed** of the flying banana. **Inertia** is the reason the banana got sliced. Inertia is the resistance to change in the **state of motion**. In other words, an object in **motion** will stay in motion, and an object at **rest** will stay at rest—unless an outside **force** acts upon it. (Try using it as an excuse the next time you want to sleep late.)

The knife and banana both have inertia. The banana was moving, and it wanted to stay moving. The knife was still (as long as your helper wasn't ducking) and wanted to stay still, or at rest. Because the knife comes down to a sharp point, or a **wedge**, it separates the banana into two pieces. That way, the banana stays moving, and the knife stays still. If you hit your helper, the banana may splat but it won't split, because your helper is not a wedge.

Eggs Over Easy

Use a broom and a glass of water to save an egg from the crushing force of gravity.

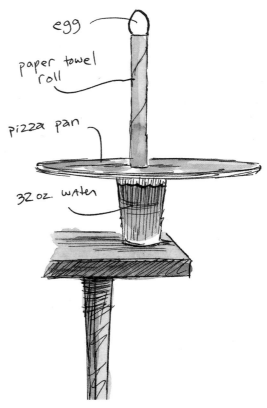

egg

paper towel roll

pizza pan

32 oz. water

What You Need

- Outside table
- 32-ounce plastic cup
- Water
- Pizza pan with no lip
- Empty toilet paper tube or paper towel roll
- Raw eggs
- Broom

What You Do

1. Clear off the table. Fill the plastic cup with water and place it near the edge of the table.

2. Center the pizza pan on top of the cup. Stand the toilet paper tube on top of the pizza pan directly over the cup of water. Stand an egg up in the end of the toilet paper tube. (See illustration.)

3. You're going to place one foot on the bristles of the broom and pull the handle toward your body. Let go of the broom with your hand, and it will fly away from you. Bend it far enough so that the broom moves quickly when you let go with your hand. Practice this

a few times, well away from the table, before continuing the experiment.

4. Place the bristles of the broom on the floor, in line with the edge of the pizza pan.

5. Now, bend the broom and let it go. What happened? Did the egg survive? Try the experiment again. You might sacrifice an egg or two, but it's all in the name of science.

What's Going On?

You might have already guessed that this experiment has to do with **inertia**. Besides inertia, there are several other concepts at work. This activity brings together many different science concepts into one. While it may seem simple to an observer, this is a very complex activity. Be proud that you got it to work.

As long as the pizza pan and toilet paper tube were moved out of the way quickly, the inertia of the egg kept it in place. So, it dropped into the glass of water and didn't break. When you bent the broom, you were storing **energy** in the bristles as **potential** **energy**. When you let the broom handle go, you released the energy that was stored in the bristles. A **collision** occurred between the broom and the pizza pan, and the egg dropped straight down into the glass of water. The egg hit the water and stopped as the water applied an upward force.

> **SAFETY:** Some raw eggs contain salmonella bacteria that will make you ill. Wash your hands thoroughly with soap and water after performing this experiment and any time you handle raw eggs.

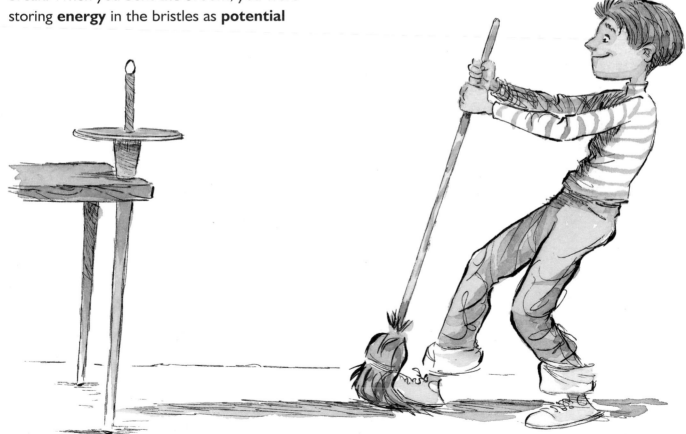

19

Cherry Tomato Fling

If you *simultaneously* drop a tomato and launch a tomato horizontally, which turns into ketchup first?

What You Do

1. Place the ruler at an angle on the edge of the table. One end of the ruler should be touching the edge of the table. The other end should be at least 4 inches away from the edge. Put one tomato between the edge of the ruler and the edge of the table. Put the other tomato against the ruler so it's far away from the table's edge (see illustration at left).

2. With one hand, hold the ruler tightly to the edge of the tabletop. To launch the tomatoes, use your other hand to push the ruler toward the edge of the table. One tomato will fall off the edge, and the other will be launched horizontally.

3. Which hit the ground first? Or did they hit at the same time? Try the experiment again with different sized objects. For instance, try using a quarter and a dime, or a tomato and a nickel.

What's Going On?

You've seen many things launched, but have you ever stopped to notice what is happening? Snowballs, softballs, kick balls, and even cherry tomatoes can all be **projectiles**. A projectile is something which is propelled by an outside **force** acting upon it. Rockets, planes, and helicopters are not projectiles, since they have a means of propelling themselves (engines).

When a projectile is launched, it forms a path called a **trajectory**. After the tomatoes are launched from the table, the only forces that affect them are **gravity** and **air resistance**. Because these objects have a small **mass** and aren't moving very quickly, they have very little air resistance, so we can ignore that. (But in other cases, you can't ignore air resistance). Gravity pulls all things down at the same **acceleration** if air resistance isn't affecting them. Since gravity is the only major force acting on the tomatoes, they should hit the ground at the same time.

This only works when projectiles are launched horizontally. We'll launch more things later at different angles and see what happens.

The Incredible Can Smasher

Crush a soft drink can with your brain...and a brick.

What You Need

- Outdoor area
- Empty drink can
- Brick
- Step stool

What You Do

1. Go outside where you can make a mess. Set the brick on top of the can. What happens?

2. Take the brick off the can and stand on the step stool. (Standing on the stool protects your feet—don't skip this part.) Drop the brick from your eye level and hit the top of the can. What happens?

3. Recycle the can. (Save the environment.)

What's Going On?

When you set the brick on the can, nothing happens. But when the brick is dropped, the can gets smashed. The can is strong enough to hold the brick when it is placed on the can; the can has **inertia** and wants to stay **stationary**. When the brick is falling, though, it also has inertia. Its inertia wants it to stay moving. And the brick is heavier than the can, so its inertia carries a greater **force**. This is what smashes the can. Inertia works with both moving and non-moving objects.

Exploding Marshmallows

Make a monster marshmallow with your microwave.

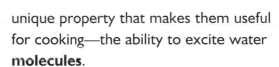

What You Need

- Marshmallows
- Plate
- Microwave oven
- Bar of soap (optional)

What You Do

1. Make sure you get a parent's permission before doing this experiment. Place a marshmallow on a plate in a microwave. Turn the microwave on for 30 seconds. Watch what happens.

2. Change the time you microwave the marshmallow and see what happens. Be careful: the marshmallow will be very hot when done.

3. Ask a parent's permission to repeat this experiment with a bar of soap. The microwave will smell like soap after you finish. But not forever.

What's Going On?

Microwaves are a type of **electromagnetic wave**. (Other types of electromagnetic waves are: **visible light**, **ultraviolet light**, **radio waves**, and **X-rays**.) Microwaves have a unique property that makes them useful for cooking—the ability to excite water **molecules**.

Microwaves cause the water molecules in your food to spin. As the molecules spin faster, they heat up. The hot water molecules then cause the food to heat up.

Food must have water (moisture) in it in order to cook in the microwave oven. Dehydrated foods, empty containers, and uncooked rice won't ever cook in the microwave, because they have no moisture.

When things heat up, they expand. As the marshmallow heats up, the tiny bubbles of moist air trapped inside grow, and the marshmallow gets big—very big. What did you see on the surface of the marshmallow after it was heated? Why do you think it only reached a certain size?

Egg Toss

Play a game of catch with a raw egg.

What You Need

- Two friends
- Old bed sheet
- Several eggs
- Outdoor area

What You Do

1. Have your friends hold the sheet perpendicular to the ground. They should hold their hands so that the sheet forms a J when viewed from the side. (See illustration.) This is to catch the egg after it hits the sheet.

2. Stand back, wind up, and throw the egg into the middle of the sheet. Try not to hit your friends. Observe what happens.

3. Switch positions with your friends so that everybody can give it a try. A stray egg might hit the ground and break, so be prepared to clean it up.

What's Going On?

Have you ever trapped a soccer ball? Or bunted a softball? Rolled after hitting the ground while diving for a catch? In all these cases, you're experiencing a **change in momentum**.

Whether the egg hits the sheet or hits a wall, the egg has to stop. In each case, the egg loses all its **momentum** as it stops. The egg will break if it doesn't have enough time to decrease its **force** before it comes to a stop. The sheet allows the egg to stop slowly compared to when the egg hits a wall or the ground. The total **impulse** is equal to the change in the egg's momentum. (Impulse equals force multiplied by **time**.) Using the sheet increases the time it takes the **egg** to stop; the force on the egg decreases, and it survives the **collision**. Air bags in automobiles work using the same physics principle and have saved many lives because of it.

Super Double Ball Launch

Make a ball bounce really high by bouncing it off another ball.

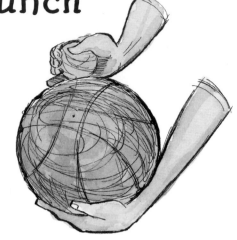

What You Need

- Outdoor area
- High-bouncing rubber ball
- Basketball

What You Do

1. Find an outside area to do this activity. Using two hands, hold the bouncy ball on top of the basketball. (See illustration top right.)

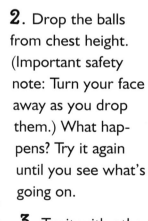

2. Drop the balls from chest height. (Important safety note: Turn your face away as you drop them.) What happens? Try it again until you see what's going on.

3. Try it with other types of balls. What happens when you switch balls?

What's Going On?

You made the high-bouncing ball even more super bouncy and probably had to go chase it down. That's the science of **collisions**.

Collisions are governed by two major scientific principles: **energy** and **momentum**. Momentum is the product of **mass** and **velocity** (**speed** in a particular direction) and must be **conserved**. (That means the momentum can't just disappear.) The basketball has a great deal of momentum as it falls because of its large mass. When the basketball collides with the ground, some momentum goes into the ground.

The remaining momentum in the basketball has now changed direction. The basketball's momentum is transferred to the bouncy ball, and watch out! The bouncy ball takes off because of its small mass. A smaller mass means it gains a greater velocity. Where else do you see small objects really take off?

Double Fisted

Use the science of vertical and horizontal force to overpower an adult.

What You Do

1. Have your adult helper make two fists and stack one on top of the other. Then, have him extend his arms until his elbows are straight (or as straight as possible). His goal is to keep his fists together. You're going to knock his fists apart using just your fingertips.

2. Keeping your hands open, place the fingers of each hand on the back of each of your helper's hands. (See illustration.) Use your fingertips to give him a very quick sideways push. Make sure you push his fists in opposite directions. His fists will **separate**.

3. Tell your adult helper to press his fists together even harder and try it again. Is it easier or harder for you this time?

What's Going On?

When your unsuspecting prey holds his fists together, he will press his fists against each other using **vertical forces**. The vertical forces of his top hand pressing down and his bottom hand pressing up cancel each other out, balancing the forces. **Balanced forces** will cause objects to maintain the same state of **motion** (in this case, **rest**). His vertical forces push only up and down. You push sideways. Since his hands are applying vertical forces, he can't balance out your horizontal finger force, and his hands slide off each other. The harder he tries to hold his fists together, the easier it is for you to do!

Fettuccine Bridge Is Falling Down

Build an incredibly strong bridge with 20 pieces of pasta.
Then try to destroy it.

What You Need

- 20 pieces of fettuccine
- Toy car
- Wood glue or tape
- Scissors
- Books

What You Do

1. You're going to build the strongest bridge possible using only 20 pieces of pasta. Here are the ground rules for this challenge. You can cut the pasta into any size pieces that you want. Your bridge should be able to hold a toy car at least 1 inch off the tabletop and, like a regular bridge, should have an opening underneath to drive the toy car under.

2. Glue or tape your pasta bridge together. If you use glue, let it dry completely before you test the bridge.

3. Now for the fun part! Slowly put one book at a time on top of the bridge until it smashes.

4. Try another design and see if you can make a stronger bridge. Challenge your friends to see who can build the strongest one.

What's Going On?

Bridge design is about strength and the amount of material you use. You probably found out that **trusses** work the best. Trusses are the triangular parts of the bridge. Triangles are often used in building because they spread out the **force** (the weight of the books). **Gravity** pulls the books straight down. The triangles redirect that **vertical force**, spreading it out **horizontally**. This distributes the force of the weight more evenly over the supports of the bridge, allowing you to make a stronger bridge using less material. As you walk around your town, take a look at the supports on bridges. See if you can find better ways to build your bridge.

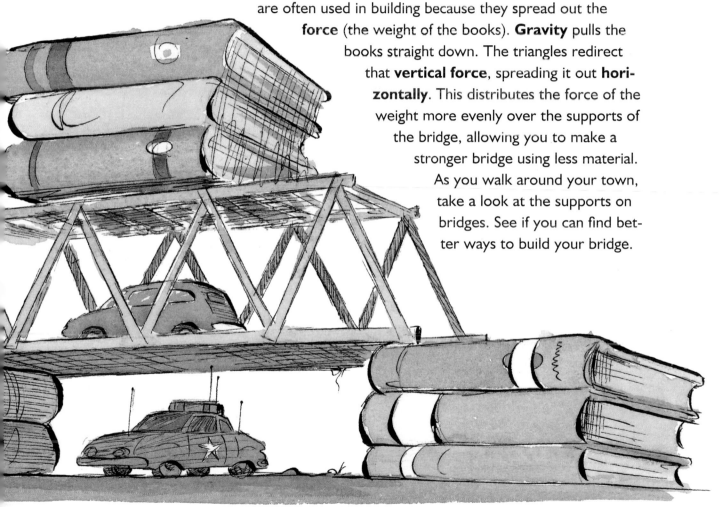

Paper Cup Crunch

Crush a cup with single step and then dance on top of a dozen.

What You Need

- A package of small paper cups
- 2 or more pieces of plywood or strong cardboard,
  2 feet square
- Step ladder
- A package of medium-sized plastic cups (optional)

What You Do

1. Place a paper cup on the floor upside down and step on it. It crunches, right? In this experiment, you'll figure out how to stand on paper cups without crunching them.

2. Arrange paper cups upside down in a 6-cup by 6-cup square. The cup rims should be touching.

3. Place the plywood square on top of the cups. Now step gently onto the center of the plywood. What happens? Did the cups crunch? If so, make a larger square to support your weight. Once the cups support your weight, go to step 4.

4. Stack a second layer of cups upside down on top of the plywood. Use the same number of cups as you did for the first layer. Add another piece of plywood and gently step onto the center of it. What happens?

5. Continue adding layers of cups and plywood to see how high you can go. Use the step ladder to get on top of the platform. Be careful!

What's Going On?

A single paper cup will never support your **weight**. So how come half a dozen paper cups do? It's because your weight is spread over all the cups. It's all about **pressure**. The mathematical calculation for pressure is the force divided by area (**P=F/A**). The **force** is your weight, which does not change during the experiment. The **area** is the flat space over which the force acts, like the soles of your foot in a footprint. The plywood helps to spread the force out to all the cups. The pressure on each cup will be less than what is needed to crush it. Your individual force (weight) determines how many cups you'll need.

Plastic cups are even stronger than paper. Try stepping very gently on just one plastic cup. Does it crunch? How many plastic cups does it take to support you? Don't forget to use the plywood platforms when you step on more than one cup.

Water Bucket Flip

Turn a bucket full of water upside down over your head without getting wet.

What You Need

- Outdoor area
- Bathing suit or raincoat (optional)
- Sturdy bucket with a handle
- Water

What You Do

1. You'll probably get a little wet, so do this activity outside. Fill the bucket about half full of water.

2. Start swinging the bucket back and forth like a pendulum.

3. When you are going at a good speed, continue to swing the bucket all the way around. You can continue for several more swings. What happens?

4. Be careful when you stop, because you'll probably get wet. If you don't want to get wet and you're outside and away from anything breakable like a window, you could just let go of the bucket. It will travel in a straight line from whatever point you let it go. Watch where it lands.

What's Going On?

Anytime you move in circles, there is a **force** present called **centripetal force**. Centripetal force is related to **speed**, which is why you have to swing the bucket quickly. According to **Newton's First Law of Motion**, an object will continue moving in a straight line unless forced to change direction. The bucket can't go in a straight line, because your arm makes it circle around you. As it's spinning around you, the bottom of the bucket applies a force to the water, trying to push it out of the bucket. Due to **Newton's Third Law of Motion** (every **action** has an equal and opposite **reaction**), the water pushes back against the bottom of the bucket, and therefore it doesn't fall out.

You feel the same effect when you round a corner quickly in a car. The car presses in on you, and your body naturally presses back on the car. You feel a force outward because the car supplied an inward force. The car pushes in on you to make you go around the corner. Because of Newton's Third Law, your body pushes back.

Scrambled Test Dummies

Test the laws of inertia with a crack team of experts.

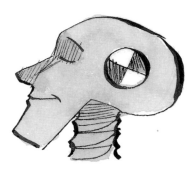

What You Need

- Several large rubber bands
- Eggs
- Large toy car
- Board to use as a ramp (2 to 6 feet long)
- Books
- Wall

What You Do

1. Use one large rubber band to secure the egg to the roof of the car.

2. Lay one end of the board against a wall that can be easily cleaned. Set up a ramp by piling the books under the other end of the board to prop it up. Place the car at the top of the ramp and let it go.

SAFETY: Some raw eggs contain salmonella bacteria that will make you ill. Wash your hands thoroughly with soap and water after performing this experiment and any time you handle raw eggs.

3. If the egg survived the crash, raise the ramp by adding more books. If your egg crashed into the wall, make a better seat belt by using two or three rubber bands at different angles to hold a new egg to the car. Keep experimenting until you run out of eggs. For even more fun, try this without any rubber bands at all, or smash two cars together while each has an egg along for the ride.

What's Going On?

The car and the egg both have **inertia**, which is an object's tendency to stay in **motion** unless acted upon by an outside **force**. The wall is the outside force that makes the car stop, but the egg still has its inertia, so it wants to continue moving in the same direction and at the same **speed** as it has been. Unless adequately restrained by the rubber bands, the egg moves forward and crashes into the wall.

Normally, when you come to a stop in a vehicle it's done gradually. **Friction** between your body and the seat supplies the force to stop you. In a car you have seat belts to help out when the car stops too quickly for your friction alone to keep you in place (such as during an emergency stop or a collision). The rubber band is a seat belt for the egg. How well did it keep the egg in place?

Why don't buses have seat belts?

You probably ride a school bus every day. Have you ever worried about the lack of seatbelts? Well, you don't have to worry—so long as you stay in your seat. The friction between your body and the seat will keep you in place anytime the bus comes to a normal, gradual stop. If the bus comes to a very quick stop though, your friction won't stop you. That's why buses have high padded seats. The padding increases the **time** it takes your body to stop in a **collision**, which decreases the force you feel. (To really get a feel for this principle, how about throwing some eggs around? See page 24.)

Skateboard Science

Dude, skateboarding is, like, science.

What You Need

- Protective gear
- Level floor, driveway, or sidewalk
- 2 skateboards
- Friend
- Rope (5 or 6 feet long)

What You Do

1. Suit up! Put on your protective gear (helmets and knee pads) before you start this experiment.

2. Place the skateboards end to end. You sit on one and have your friend sit on the other so you are facing each other. Using your open palms, push off each other. What happens?

3. Now sit facing each other with a piece of rope between you. Leave an opening of 4 or 5 feet between you. What will happen when you both pull on the rope? What will happen when only one of you pulls on the rope? Try it and see.

4. Try this in an open area. Stand on your skateboard by yourself. Step off your skateboard. What happens? Do it again, but this time step off faster. Watch the skateboard shoot off, no rope or friend needed.

What's Going On?

In the first two cases, you and your friend were initially **stationary**. That means that your **momentum** was zero. Momentum must be conserved in all interactions, according to the **Law of Conservation of Momentum**. Therefore after the movement (resulting from pushing off each other), the total momentum must still be zero! If you and your friend were moving, how can those two momenta add up to zero? The secret is direction; you were moving in opposite directions, but each had the same momentum. It's like adding +5 and -5 in math; they add up to zero. In step 2, when you pulled on the rope, only you had momentum and so you moved closer to your friend.

When you step off the skateboard quickly, the board shoots off the other way. The board had the same momentum as you, but in the opposite direction. Then why does the board move so fast? Because you apply **force**. It's like how passengers stepping off a boat actually push the boat away from the dock (that's why they tie it to the dock). Have you ever stepped out of a canoe? Same thing happens.

Egg Crusher

Squeeze an egg one way, and you can't crush it—no matter how hard you try. Do it another way to get raw egg in your hand.

What You Need

- Your amazing strength
- A raw egg (or two)

What You Do

1. Using your thumb and forefinger, squeeze the top and bottom of the egg as hard as you can. What happens?

2. Place the egg in the palm of your hand and wrap your fingers around the middle of the egg as tight as you can. Squeeze. Does the egg break?

3. Hold the egg in your palm again, but press all four of your fingers just on the opposite side of the egg. Do not tighten your hand as you did in step 2. Squeeze the egg with just your fingertips. What happens?

SAFETY: Some raw eggs contain salmonella bacteria that will make you ill. Wash your hands thoroughly with soap and water after performing this experiment and any time you handle raw eggs.

What's Going On?

When you first tried to break the egg with your thumb and forefinger, you pushed on the top and bottom of the egg. The egg has more strength here than anywhere else, because the eggshell forms an **arch** at these two points. The curved shape of an arch gives it great strength. The arch is able to support weight pressing down on it by spreading the weight out along the entire arch. The **force** radiates throughout the arch, lessening the force's impact.

You will see arches used in church doorways, under older bridges, and even on ancient monuments like the famous Pantheon in Rome, built in 27 BCE. (Which makes you wonder: Did architects look at the egg for design tips?)

When you try to break the egg from the side in steps 2 and 3, the secret is **pressure**. In step 2, you spread out the force of your hand over a large **area**. (Remember, pressure equals force divided by area.) Therefore, the pressure isn't great enough to break the egg's shell. When you decrease the area in step 3 by only pressing on part of the egg, you can break it.

Why do eggs crack so easily? The eggshell's material, calcium carbonate, is strong enough to withstand a mother hen sitting on top of it, but thin enough for a chick to break out of it with its sharp beak. Force and pressure, and where you strike an egg, all help determine if or how it cracks.

When you crack an egg to cook it, you hit it against a sharp corner so it cracks. (Again, the pressure is greater because the area the force acts on is smaller.) If you have small hands, you might actually break the egg in step 2 because your fingers don't reach all the way around the egg. Challenge a parent or a friend to try this. Remember, you know the secret.

Leaning Tower of Nickels

Knock the bottom nickel out of a stack without knocking the stack over.

What You Need

- 15 nickels*
- Butter knife
- Additional coins (optional)

*You can use any coins for this experiment, as long as they are all the same kind.

What You Do

1. Stack 15 nickels in a tower. Make the sides as straight as possible.

2. Use the butter knife to knock out the bottom nickel. What happens?

3. Make an even taller stack of nickels. How high can you go before the tower crashes when you knock out the bottom nickel?

What's Going On?

Inertia is the resistance to change in the **motion** of an object. The inertia of an object is directly related to **mass**, so the more coins there are, the greater the mass and the easier this activity is to do. But you eventually reach a height where **stability** is an issue. You also have to perform the activity fast enough so that **friction** between the coins is not a factor. Friction decreases **speed**.

The One-Handed, Two-Person Topple

Knock your friends out—uh, I mean over—with this experiment.

What You Need

- 6 to 8 feet of strong rope
- 2 friends

What You Do

1. Give the rope to your friends. Have them play Tug of War. Warn them that, with just one hand, you may bring them both crashing to the ground.

2. When your friends are tugging on the rope, stand between them and push downward on the rope. Do your friends tumble to the ground? At the very least, they'll be forced to move closer to each other.

3. Have your friends pull even harder. Push down on the middle of the rope again.

What's Going On?

When your friends pull on the rope, they pull with a **horizontal force** only. If they are of similar strength, the force of one of them pulling on the rope is **counteracted** by the force of the other one pulling. But when you push down on the middle of the rope, you add a **vertical force**. This makes the rope pull down at an angle. Your friends react to the new force, which is why they move down and toward each other.

Parachuting Eggs

Build a parachute to save your eggs from being scrambled.

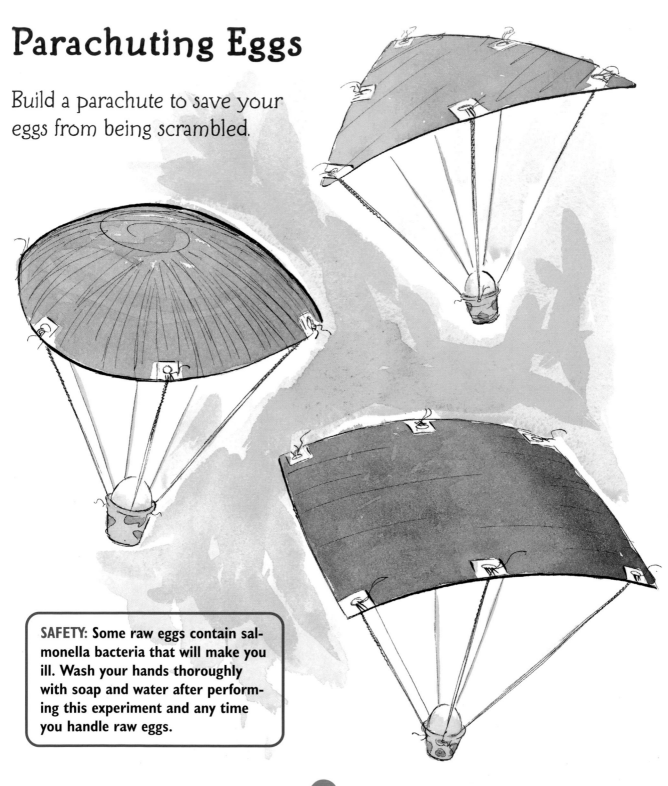

What You Do

1. You're going to design and test different parachutes in order to save an egg from getting smashed. The size of the parachute will depend on the height from which you drop it; you might have to make larger parachutes if you want to drop eggs from a greater height.

2. Cut a 12-inch circle, a 12-inch triangle, and a 12-inch square from the plastic bag. These will be your parachutes. Use the hole punch to make six holes an equal distance around the edge of each parachute. Tie a 12-inch long piece of string to each hole. You might need to use tape to reinforce the punched openings in the bag.

3. Poke six holes an equal distance around the lip of the small cup and tie the other end of each string to the cup. This cup will serve as your cradle for the egg, so put your egg in the cup and get ready to test your parachutes.

Drop the parachutes from a high point (raise them over your head, drop them from the deck, etc.) Which parachute worked the best? (If the eggs keep bouncing out of the cup when the parachutes land, use the tape to hold the eggs in the cup.)

4. Cut small holes near the top (center) of the parachutes. Does that make a difference?

What's Going On?

You've probably seen dandelion seeds floating to the ground after the wind that carried them has died. They drift slowly because they have reached **terminal velocity**. At terminal velocity, objects are no longer experiencing **acceleration**. When **gravity** begins to pull an object down, the object accelerates at a constant rate until it reaches terminal velocity. Terminal velocity is created by **air resistance**, which is the **friction** created as the air pushes on the surface. As an object falls faster, it hits more air particles and has more air resistance. Eventually, it will have enough air resistance pushing up to balance the **weight** pushing down. At this point, the object will stop accelerating and fall the rest of the way at a constant **velocity** (its terminal velocity). An object's terminal velocity depends upon its shape and its weight. The average person's terminal velocity is about 120 mph (lying flat), while an ant's is so low that she can survive a fall from any height!

Egg Drop (Let's Get Crackin')

Design and build a contraption that will save a raw egg from smashing.

What You Need

- Raw eggs
- Various materials found around the house
- Outdoor area

What You Do

1. This activity is a challenge to save the eggs. Find a suitable elevated location that is safe to stand on, and that you can clean up if the egg doesn't survive (boo-hoo). You can use a deck, or you could even stand on a chair.

2. Design and build a contraption that will allow the egg to survive the fall when you drop it. Can you make a cradle with lots of padding? How about something with springs on it? (No parachutes this time—that's on page 42.) What works best?

3. Drop the egg from different heights. Does it survive?

What's Going On?

You probably broke a few eggs, but that's okay. Trial and error is the appropriate way to perform scientific experiments.

What gave you the best results? Was it a design using a material that crushed and could only be used once? How did very sturdy and rigid materials work?

The key to saving the egg is **time**. You want to increase the time between the **collision** (when the contraption hits the ground) and when the egg feels the impact. The added time decreases the **force** of the egg's impact.

Defying Gravity

Drop a key ring and watch it not crash to the Earth.

What You Need

- Key ring full of keys
- Long shoelace
- Pencil

What You Do

1. Remove one key from the key ring. Tie it to one end of the shoelace, and tie the key ring (with the other keys still on it) to the other end.

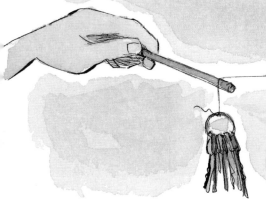

2. Drape the string over the pencil. The key ring should hang down about 1 inch below the pencil. Hold the key in your other hand. (See illustration.)

3. Let go of the key. What happens? Do it again, watching the path of the key very carefully. Wow! This is the perfect trick to amaze your friends and family.

What's Going On?

The key to this trick is **energy**. There are two different types of energy at work. Energy of **motion** is **kinetic energy**. Stored energy is called **potential energy**. When both the key ring and the key are **stationary**, they have potential energy. The key ring has more potential energy than the key because it has more **mass** (due to the additional keys). When you let go of the single key, it falls a long distance, building up **momentum** and **speed** as it travels, so it has a lot of kinetic

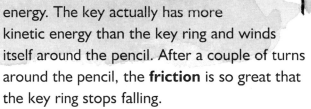

energy. The key actually has more kinetic energy than the key ring and winds itself around the pencil. After a couple of turns around the pencil, the **friction** is so great that the key ring stops falling.

The cool thing about the two types of energy is that they can go back and forth. For instance, potential energy is converted into kinetic energy every time you swing on a swing set. The potential energy at the top of your swing is converted into kinetic energy at the bottom of your swing.

Water Balloon Launcher

Build a gigantic slingshot, launch a water balloon, and make a big splash!

What You Need

- Scissors
- Plastic wrap
- 6 feet of surgical tubing
- Balloons
- Water
- 2 friends
- Large outdoor area

What You Do

1. To build the slingshot, cut a 6-foot long piece of plastic wrap and lay it down on the ground. Knot the ends of the surgical tubing together. Lay it down on top of the plastic wrap. Stretch the ends of the tubing apart so it forms the outline of a long, skinny hot dog. The sides should be about 6 inches apart. (See illustration.) Wrap the plastic wrap around the tubing several times, so that it makes a membrane in between the edges of the tubing. Make sure the sides of the tubing stay about 6 inches apart.

2. Fill up several balloons with water and tie them off. (Half-filled balloons work the best.) Take your slingshot and the water balloons outside.

3. Have each of your friends hold one end of the surgical tubing. Hold the ends of the tubing so that the plastic wrap membrane is in the middle. Aiming away from any windows, hold a water balloon against the plastic wrap and pull the balloon back. Let it fly! How big of a splash does it make?

4. Now try to make the biggest splash you can. Try pulling the slingshot back farther. Or change the angle at which you launch the balloon. How high can you get the balloon to go? How far can you get it to fly? What makes the biggest splash?

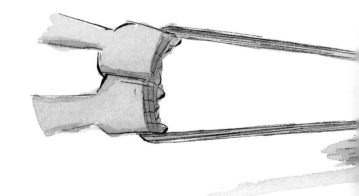

What's Going On?

You've stretched rubber bands before and felt them snap back. Now you've just made a giant rubber band that will snap back. But as it snaps back it's going to launch water balloons. This is how it works: **elastic** materials return to their original size after they've been stretched because they obey **Newton's Third Law** (for every **action** there is an opposite and equal **reaction**). So when you pull the plastic wrap on your slingshot back and let it go, it bounces back to its original position, hurling the balloon forward.

The balloon becomes a **projectile** as it hurtles through the air. A projectile is an object that after being launched has no way to create its own **force**. **Gravity** soon starts tugging it down. (Gravity is the only major force acting on the balloon. The **air resistance** isn't strong.) The balloon will follow the same general path (called a **parabola)** every time it is launched. But you can affect how high and how far a water balloon flies by changing the angle at which the balloon is launched.

Based on your experiments, what angle gives you the greatest distance? What angle gives the greatest height?

Up, Up & Away

Can you build your own hot air balloon with a trash bag?

What You Need

- Large trash bag
- Cellophane tape
- Blow dryer
- Outdoor area with an electrical socket nearby

What You Do

1. To make the hot air balloon, place the opening of the bag around your fist and gather it down, but not too tight. Wrap the cellophane tape around the opening. (Make sure that your hand can easily come out.) The opening MUST be larger than the nozzle of the blow dryer.

2. Go outside and hold the blow dryer about 3 inches away from the opening in the trash bag. Turn it on. Watch as the bag begins to inflate. Be careful not to let the blow dryer touch the bag, or the plastic may melt.

3. As the bag begins to fill, keep the nozzle of the blow dryer pointing up and hold the bag above the blow dryer. One hand should be on the bag and one on the blow dryer.

4. Let go of the balloon and watch it rise. Try to keep the blow dryer under the opening as long as possible.

What's Going On?

Helium balloons and hot air balloons like the one you made use similar scientific principles. They both float on the air and are at the mercy of the air.

Balloons float because of a difference in **density**. Density is the amount of **mass** (**weight**) in a certain **volume** (space). Helium is less dense than air, meaning 1 kilogram of helium will take up more space than 1 kg of air. That's why a helium balloon will float so easily—it's less dense than the air around it.

The hot air balloon requires some work to float. As you heat the air with the blow dryer, the air **molecules** move faster, and some escape out of the opening in the bottom of your balloon. This makes the hot air in the balloon less dense than the air that surrounds it, causing a **buoyant force** upward (from the outside air). Buoyant force is due to the difference in **pressure** on the top and bottom of an object. (It's what keeps you afloat in a swimming pool.) The buoyant force is greater than the force of **gravity**, so the balloon rises. As the air inside the balloon cools, it gets denser and the balloon gradually begins to fall.

Large hot air balloons (the kind you can ride) have a propane gas heater, which the pilot turns on and off to control the altitude.

It's Not a Shoe Box! It's a Catapult!

Use simple objects to build a grape-launching catapult.

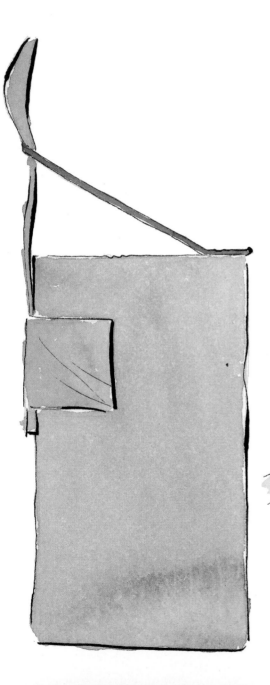

What You Need

- Duct or packing tape
- Long plastic spoon
- Shoebox
- Rubber bands
- Grapes (or any small item to launch)
- Outdoor area

What You Do

1. Tape the bottom of the spoon to the end of a shoebox. The concave part of the spoon should face along the side of the box (see illustration).

2. Loop one end the rubber band around the spoon and the tape the rubber band to the middle of the spoon. Tape the other end of the rubber band to the side of the shoebox (see illustration). Make sure you've got a good stretch on your rubber band, so there's tension. (To increase tension, use a smaller rubber band, or loop it around the spoon a couple of times.)

3. Use one hand to hold the shoebox. Use the other hand to load the grape on the spoon and pull back on the spoon. Let it go and launch the grape. How far did the grape go?

4. Adjust the position of the rubber band so it stretches farther, creating greater tension. How does this change the launch? What happens if you use more than one rubber band?

What's Going On?

Whether they're built to launch grapes at targets or boulders at castle walls, all **catapults** work because of **elastic** materials. Here, you're using the elasticity of the rubber band to store **energy** in your catapult. You put the energy in the rubber band by pulling the spoon back with your hand. That energy goes into the grape and becomes **kinetic energy**. So the grape flies! Stretching the rubber band more stores more energy and makes the grape fly farther. Using two rubber bands increases the energy storage capacity and makes the grape fly even farther.

In a castle-busting catapult like the one below, a pulley and rope system does the same work as your hand did on the spoon. A quick release of the rope launches the boulder at the unlucky target!

The Flying Marshmallow Machine

Launch marshmallows at a target. Who knew clothespins could be so much fun?

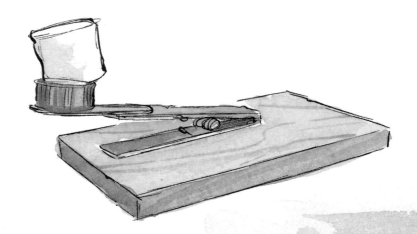

What You Need

- Glue
- Spring-style clothespin
- Tongue depressor
- Small scrap of wood
- Plastic drink bottle top
- Marshmallows
- Marker
- Newspaper

What You Do

1. To make the machine that will make marshmallows fly, glue the clothespin to one end of the tongue depressor (see illustration at right). Glue the other side of the clothespin to the scrap of wood. Glue the bottle cap to the raised end of the tongue depressor, near to but not right at the end. Let the glue dry.

2. Place the catapult on a sturdy table. Put a marshmallow in the bottle cap to load the catapult for its trial run. Press down on the end of the tongue depressor and launch. What happens?

3. Use the marker to draw a target on the newspaper. Put it on the floor, about 10 feet away from the catapult. Challenge a friend to a contest to see who can land a marshmallow closest to the bull's-eye. To change the angle of the marshmallow's trajectory, experiment with raising one end of the base of the catapult.

What's Going On?

Your machine is a type of **catapult**. The key to this catapult lies in the metal coil at the center of the clothespin. That makes it a **torsion catapult**. *Torsion* comes from the word **torque**, and torque is a **rotational force**.

Torque is what allows you to fling the marshmallow so high and far. When you press down a little bit on the tongue depressor, the torque multiplies your force and stores it in the coil. The coil is **elastic**, so when you move your finger, it springs back, launching the marshmallow.

But torque isn't just for catapults. You actually benefit from it every day. Whenever you open a door, you're taking advantage of the torque in the hinges. The next time you push open a door, put your hand close to the hinges and try to open it. It won't work, because you need more torque. This is also what makes it more fun to sit at end of a see-saw than in the middle.

Balloon Dragster

Build a dragster with a piece of cardboard, straw, and a balloon. Experiment with different shapes and sizes of balloons to see what makes your dragster fastest.

What You Need

- Piece of cardboard, 6 x 10 inches
- Scissors
- 4 straight pins
- Colored markers or crayons (optional)
- Flexible straw
- Tape
- Balloons (un-inflated)

What You Do

1. First you'll make the dragster parts. Cut a 3 x 4-inch piece of cardboard. This will be the body of your dragster. Cut four circles, each with a 2-inch diameter, for wheels. Use a pin to poke a hole in the center of each wheel

and then set the wheels aside. Decorate your dragster parts if you want. (See illustration.)

2. Bend the flexible straw into an L-shape. Lay it lengthwise in the middle of the dragster's body, with the straw's mouth-end sticking up near the front of the car and the opposite end extending past the rear of the car (see illustration). Tape the straw in place.

3. Put the mouth of the balloon over the mouth of the straw. Tape it in place. Just to test your tape job, blow into the open end of the straw to make sure you can inflate the balloon. If it fails, try re-taping the balloon to the straw.

4. Attach the wheels to the dragster body using a pin for each wheel. Test it to make sure it rolls. Make adjustments if you need to.

5. Blow into the straw until the balloon is half full of air. As you take your mouth off the straw, quickly block the end of the straw with your finger to keep the air in. Then let go of the straw and watch the dragster take off.

6. Try different sizes and shapes of balloons, and vary the amount of air in the balloons. Build two so you and a friend can race them. Test out other modifications, such as changing the size of the wheels or the shape of the body. Can you make your dragster faster?

What's Going On?

Dragsters are a special kind of race car. They use the principles of rocket science to move in a straight line as fast as possible, and so did you when you built and tested your dragster.

Rocket engines and balloon dragsters work according to **Newton's Third Law of Motion**. That law says that for every **action** (**force**) there is an equal and opposite **reaction** (force). In your dragster, the balloon pushes air through the straw—action—so the dragster moves forward—opposite reaction.

Are you wondering how the forces end up being equal? **Newton's Second Law of Motion** says that force is equal to **mass** times **acceleration**. The air rushing out of the straw has a tiny mass but a very high **acceleration**. The dragster has a larger mass, but less acceleration.

Potato Poppers

Can you create your own thunder with potato projectiles?

What You Need

- Adult helper
- 8- to 12-inch length of PVC pipe, 1 inch in diameter
- 13- or 14-inch length of a broom handle or a dowel, ¾ inch in diameter
- Potatoes
- Knife
- Outdoor area
- Marshmallows (optional)

What You Do

1. Have an adult cut the PVC pipe and broom handle or dowel to the correct lengths. Make sure the broom handle fits into the PVC pipe. Cut the potato into ½-inch thick (or less) slices.

2. Press one end of the pipe into a potato slice. Turn the pipe over and do the same on the other side. Bring your pipe and dowel to an open area.

3. To get started, push the dowel about 1 inch into the potato slice in one end of the pipe (use the ground to help if needed). Aim the popper away from people and animals.

Ready, aim, and ram the dowel all the way through. What do you see? What do you hear?

4. Repeat step 2 to reload the potato popper. Try a different thickness for your slice to see what works best. You also can try marshmallows as your projectile. Put a slice of potato on one end of the pipe and fill the other end with marshmallows.

What's Going On?

When you were a little kid did you ever play with pop guns? (You know, the toy guns that make a popping sound.) Well, you just made your own. Who knew potatoes could be so much fun?

Launching the potato slice was the result of **air pressure**. The potato slices plugging the ends of the pipe trap the air inside. As you push the dowel through, the air pressure inside the pipe increases. When the air pressure inside is great enough, the slice on the opposite end of the pipe pops out.

Sound waves are created by differences in air pressure. For instance, thunder is created by rapidly expanding air as it's heated by lightning. So you also got a popping sound as the potato slice flew out.

How far did your potato go? Did the marshmallow work better? Did either sound like thunder?

Pop Bottle Rocket

Pump up a bottle and watch it take off.

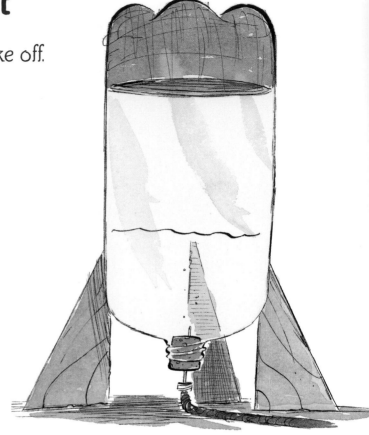

What You Need

- Bathing suit or raincoat (optional)
- Outdoor area
- Scissors
- Cardboard
- Duct tape
- Empty 2-liter bottle
- Small nail
- Cork
- Ball-inflating needle
- Bicycle tire pump

What You Do

1. You're about to get wet, so put on your bathing suit or raincoat and go outside. Cut three or four triangle-shaped fins from the cardboard. The fins are going to be used to stand the rocket up and help it fly straighter. The top of the bottle is the bottom of the rocket (see illustration). Tape the fins securely to the bottle using the duct tape.

2. With the nail, poke a tiny hole in the cork that will allow the ball-inflating needle to go all the way through the cork. Fill the bottle about $\frac{1}{3}$ full of water and insert the cork. The cork must be very snug for this to work. Attach the needle to the bicycle pump. Insert the needle and turn the rocket over so that the cork is resting on the ground.

3. Begin your countdown as you pump the bicycle pump. Keep pumping until the bottle blasts off!

4. Launch the bottle several times, changing the amount of water each time. What's the best amount of water to use?

5. Try using other size bottles. Make sure the cork is tight. Which bottles go the highest?

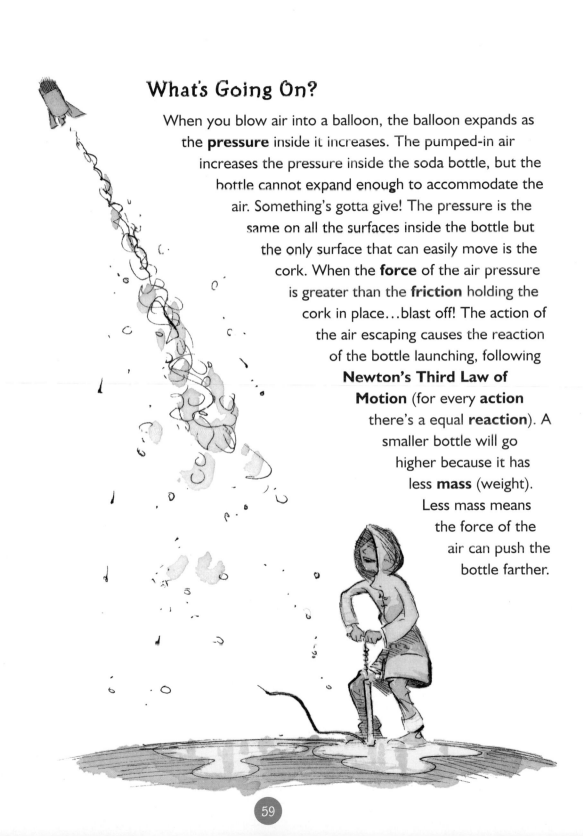

What's Going On?

When you blow air into a balloon, the balloon expands as the **pressure** inside it increases. The pumped-in air increases the pressure inside the soda bottle, but the bottle cannot expand enough to accommodate the air. Something's gotta give! The pressure is the same on all the surfaces inside the bottle but the only surface that can easily move is the cork. When the **force** of the air pressure is greater than the **friction** holding the cork in place...blast off! The action of the air escaping causes the reaction of the bottle launching, following **Newton's Third Law of Motion** (for every **action** there's a equal **reaction**). A smaller bottle will go higher because it has less **mass** (weight). Less mass means the force of the air can push the bottle farther.

Candy Rocket Engine

Instead of eating candy and drinking soda, use them to make a big mess. All in the name of science, of course.

What You Need

- Outdoor area
- Wintergreen Lifesavers
- Thin straw
- 2-liter bottle of soda

What You Do

1. This activity makes a big mess, so make sure you don't have to clean up the outdoor area you'll be using.

2. Unwrap the Lifesavers. Slide the straw through the hole of each Lifesaver, so that you have the entire package held on the straw. Stand the 2-liter bottle up in the middle of your outdoor area. Uncap the bottle.

3. Slide all of the Lifesavers off the straw down into the mouth of the bottle and back away. What happens? Try other kinds of candy.

What's Going On?

Rocket engines work by forcing a **gas** out of the nozzle in the back. You created a candy rocket engine that was actually pushing the Earth! Sodas are carbonated (containing dissolved carbon dioxide gas under **pressure**); that's what gives them their fizz. When the candy starts to dissolve, it gives the gas bubbles present in the soda something to form around. A lot of gas forms at the same time, and it explodes out of the bottle. The **momentum** of the gas (a tiny **mass**) coming out of the bottle is equal to the momentum of the bottle, which pushes the Earth (large mass) but in the opposite direction.

Triangle Glider

Make a giant glider and watch it sail.

What You Need

- 8 straws
- Tape
- Newspaper or tissue paper
- Outdoor area

What You Do

1. You're going to make a giant triangle out of straws. First, you'll make the sides of the triangle. Put three straws together by inserting them end-to-end. Repeat this with three more straws to make the

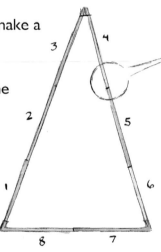

other side. Put two straws together for the bottom of the triangle. Bend 1 inch of each end of the bottom piece and insert each into one of the sides. Tape the two long side pieces together to finish the triangle frame.

2. Wrap the newspaper around the frame and tape it in place. You can wrap the paper so it covers both sides or just one. You may need several sheets to cover the frame.

3. Go outside and launch your glider. This may take some practice, so be patient. Hold the glider over your head, with your hands on the long sides, and toss it. Try it again and toss it harder. How far can you get it to fly? Build two and challenge your friends to a gliding contest.

What's Going On?

Gliders fly according to the same principle as airplanes. You supply the **force** to launch a glider the same as you do for a paper airplane. The **airfoil** of the wing allows the glider to sail on the wind. An airfoil is designed to provide **lift** using **Bernoulli's Principle**. The airfoil makes the air move faster over the top, creating a low **pressure** zone above the glider. This lifts the glider, keeping it in the air.

A **delta wing airfoil** (which is what you just made) can even be large enough to support a person, as in hang gliders. Gliders can be towed by airplanes or launched off tall cliffs. Bernoulli's Principle is at work and gives the glider lift as air rushes over the wing.

Straw Launcher

Launch a straw into the air using air pressure.

What You Need

- Empty 20-ounce plastic drink bottle
- 2 slightly different diameter straws
- Modeling clay

What You Do

1. Rinse out the bottle and let it dry. Place the smaller straw in the neck of the bottle and seal it in place using the clay. Most of the straw should extend outside of the bottle.

2. Seal one end of the larger straw with a tiny amount of the clay. Slide the open end of the larger straw over the smaller straw, and you are ready to fire.

3. Be careful to aim the rocket away from people, animals, and siblings. Smash the bottle between your hands and watch what happens.

What's Going On?

You've just built a small rocket. It works because of **air pressure**. When you place the larger straw over the smaller one, you trap air inside the bottle. The **pressure** inside is equal to the pressure outside. But you apply an **unbalanced force** when you smash the bottle, and this causes the pressure in the bottle to increase. This increased pressure is felt all over the inside of the bottle. The increased air pressure escapes by forcing the larger straw to launch. A larger unbalanced force—such as a faster, stronger compression—will cause a greater **acceleration** and higher flight of your rocket.

clay

clay

Sparking Grapes

Microwave grapes and watch the sparks fly.

What You Need

- White grapes
- Knife
- Microwave-safe plate
- Microwave oven

What You Do

1. Slice the grape down the center toward the stem, but not all the way through. The two halves should just be attached by a tiny piece of grape skin.

2. Place the two grape halves face down on the plate.

3. Set the microwave for 20 seconds. Turn it on and watch the sparks fly.

What's Going On?

A microwave oven is a very useful appliance around our house. We use it to heat and cook food. It also can give you fireworks, as you saw from this activity.

The oven produces **microwaves**, which are a type of **electromagnetic radiation**. All electromagnetic waves create a changing **electric field**, which will cause **electrons** to move. (Electrons are negatively charged particles located around the nucleus of the **atom**, and everything in the world is made up of atoms, so everything has electrons.) Moving electrons through a thin **conductor** will give you light just like a **filament** in a light bulb. In this activity, the thin flap of grape left is a conductor, and the microwaves make electrons move through it. When the grape separates, the moving electrons have created so much heat that you've burned out the grape.

Rocket-Powered Toy

Strap a rocket to your toy car.

What You Need

- Smooth, level outdoor area
- Rubber band
- Film canister
- Toy car
- Toilet paper
- Teaspoon
- Baking soda
- Vinegar or lemon juice

What You Do

1. Choose an area where you can make a mess. Strap the film canister to the top of the toy car with the rubber band. Make sure that the wheels can roll.

2. Stack two pieces of toilet paper, one on top of the other. Place 1 teaspoon of baking soda in the center of the toilet paper. Wrap it tightly around the baking soda. Fill the film canister about half full of vinegar.

3. Put the baking soda in the canister and quickly put on the cap. Step back. What happens?

4. Experiment with different amounts of baking soda and vinegar to see how fast you can get your car to go.

What's Going On?

Most rocket motors use a **chemical reaction** and that is the case with this rocket. The **reaction** of the baking soda (solid) and the vinegar (liquid) creates carbon dioxide (a gas). As the **gas** is created, the **pressure** inside the canister increases. When the pressure is great enough, the cap pops off, and your rocket-powered toy car moves. The cap and the car move because of **Newton's Third Law** (for every **action** there is an equal and opposite **reaction**). They both feel the same **force**, but the car moves slower because of its larger **mass**.

Ping-Pong Ball Launch

Launch a ping-pong ball and watch it spin out of control.

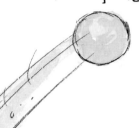

What You Need

- Empty wrapping paper cardboard tube
- Ping-pong balls (must slide into the tube easily)

What You Do

1. Hold the tube upright. Drop a ping-pong ball in it.

2. Move the tube like you're hammering a nail. You might have to change the angle to get the ball to come out. Try different angles and observe what happens. What angle gave you the best curve? Try putting two balls in at a time and see what happens.

What's Going On?

The ball will curve as it comes out of the tube. The greater the spin, the greater the curve. By changing angles, you can change the angle at which it curves. You have probably seen many balls curve as they travel; think about soccer balls, tennis balls, and softballs. The curve is created by the difference in the direction of the air after it passes over the ball. This is called the **Magnus Effect**. As the ball spins, one side is pulling the air over it and causing the wake behind the ball to be bent to that side. The other side is stopping the air, which causes the air to slow down and not bend as much. This makes the wake change direction, which in turn causes the ball to curve because its net **force** has been changed. The net force is **lift**, which can actually be in any direction. Would fuzz (ridges or seams) on the ball make it spin more or less? What would it be like to play tennis with a ping-pong ball?

Paper Helicopters

Raid your recycling bin to create a whole fleet of helicopters.

What You Need

- Scissors
- 2 straws
- Tape
- Manila file folder
- Hole punch

What You Do

1. Make the launcher first. Cut two 3-inch pieces from one straw. Tape one of the pieces to the other straw so that it extends beyond it by ¼ inch or less. Tape the other piece to the opposite side of the long straw on the same end (see illustration on the left).

2. Use the template to make your helicopter with the manila file folder. Copy or trace the diagram on page 67. Punch out two holes that match up with the two short straws on your launcher. Fold along the dotted lines.

3. Put the helicopter over your launcher, making sure that it slides freely on the straws. Spin the straws between your palms and watch the helicopter lift. Turn the helicopter over and try the other direction. Which direction works best? You might get the best results by dropping the launcher after you spin it.

4. Try different sized helicopters and raid your recycling bin for different weights of paper and cardboard (cereal boxes, juice boxes, etc.). Try bending the flaps more or less to see what gives you the best helicopter. You can even make a four-blade helicopter by attaching two rotors.

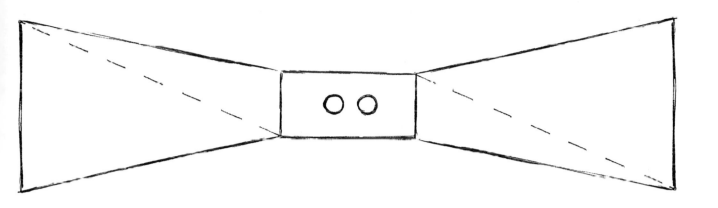

What's Going On?

To fly, helicopters use the same physics principles as planes. The rotor is just a spinning wing. The most important thing is that it's shaped like a traditional **airfoil**. The airfoil directs the movement of air over the rotor, using **Bernoulli's Principle** to create **lift**. That means the air rushing over the top of the rotor moves faster than air rushing over the bottom. The faster air creates a lower **pressure** zone above the helicopter. The lower pressure creates lift. Motorized helicopters (the kind you fly in) also have a second smaller vertical rotor which keeps the entire helicopter from spinning.

Loopy Airlines

Build a paper airplane that will fly in a circle.

What You Do

1. You're going to build a large flat-wing paper airplane to investigate flaps. Follow the illustrations to fold your airplane. (Fold the paper in half the long way and fold the corners into the center. Fold the nose in.)

2. Fold in the halves, than fold them back out to make the body of the plane very shallow, about ½ inch high. You should end up with a very flat-winged airplane. Attach the paper clip to the nose to give the plane some additional weight.

3. Make a small tear, about ½ inch long, at the back of the plane where the body and wing meet (see illustration). Fold the back ¼ inch of the the wings up into flaps. Toss the plane. What happens?

4. See if you can make the airplane complete a full loop. You can also try to make a horizontal loop.

5. Bend the flaps different ways and observe what happens.

What's Going On?

Pilots control planes with the **flaps** and **rudders**. Flaps redirect the air and change the direction of the **force** on the plane. If the flaps are bent up, you will create a force on the back of the wing, which acts down, while **lift** on the front will act up. This makes the plane climb. If you reverse the flaps, the plane will go down. Rudders work like the flaps, but they are oriented vertically, so they steer the plane right or left instead of up or down.

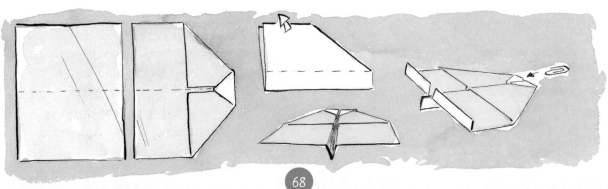

Hoopsters

Make a bizarre-looking flyer.

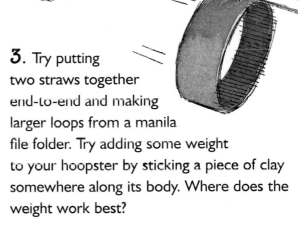

What You Need

- Scissors
- 2 index cards
- Tape
- 2 straws
- Friend (optional)
- Manila file folder (optional)
- Clay (optional)

What You Do

1. For each hoopster, cut a 1-inch strip from the short side of an index card. Roll the strip into a circle and tape it to one end of your straw. Cut a 1-inch strip from the long side of the other index card. Roll it into a larger circle and tape to the other end of your straw.

2. Hold the hoopster in the middle and toss it gently. Experiment with which end flies better. If you like, challenge a friend to build one and see whose hoopster will stay in the air longer.

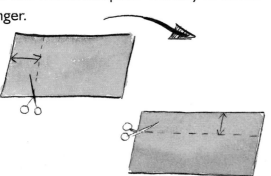

3. Try putting two straws together end-to-end and making larger loops from a manila file folder. Try adding some weight to your hoopster by sticking a piece of clay somewhere along its body. Where does the weight work best?

What's Going On?

Your hoopster is an experiment in **aerodynamics**. Aerodynamics comes from the Greek words for air and power. It's the study of how **gases** move. Air, which is a gas, lifts the hoopster as it passes over and under the loops. **Bernoulli's Principle** states that fast-moving air has a lower **pressure** than slow-moving air. The loops of the hoopster are **airfoils**. The air has to move faster over the top of the loops than it does beneath the loops. This creates a low-pressure zone above the hoopster that **lifts** it into the air. Helicopters and airplanes use this principle to fly.

Wacky Whirlybird

Make your own paper helicopter and watch it soar.

What You Need

- Scissors
- Paper
- Tape
- Paper clips

What You Do

1. To make a whirlybird, cut out the paper as the diagram shows you. Cut along the dotted lines. Fold along the solid lines.

2. Use the tape to secure the sides you folded in. (See illustration.)

3. Place the paper clip at the bottom of the whirlybird. Drop it and watch it fly. Throw it up in the air and watch what happens.

4. Try adding additional paper clips to your whirlybird. Drop it from different heights. What works best?

What's Going On?

Helicopters fly because of **Bernoulli's Principle**, which states that faster air has lower **air pressure** than slower air. As your whirlybird falls, the rotors catch and direct the wind. This causes the whirlybird to rotate. The rotors are little **airfoils** that help it fly. Airfoils are curved surfaces (like a wing or rotor); the curved top of the wing creates higher **velocity** air over the top. Helicopters that people fly in have a motor that spins the rotors. The spinning motion moves the air over the rotors. The air moves faster over the top of the rotor, so it has a lower pressure than the air underneath the rotor. This creates **lift**.

The Fastest Airplane Ever

Use a rubber band to give your airplane a boost.

What You Need

- Sheet of paper
- Scissors
- Tape
- Rubber band
- Pencil
- Yardstick
- Stopwatch

What You Do

1. With the paper, fold the classic dart paper airplane according to the illustrations below. For extra strength, fold the nose in about 1 inch.

2. Cut a slit on the bottom of the plane about 1 inch from the nose. (See illustration 6).

3. To make the launcher, tape the rubber band to the end of the pencil near the eraser.

4. Put the rubber band in the V you cut in step 2. Hold the pencil in one hand and the tail of the plane in the other. Let go of the tail and watch the plane soar.

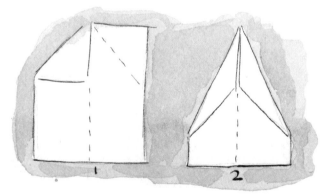

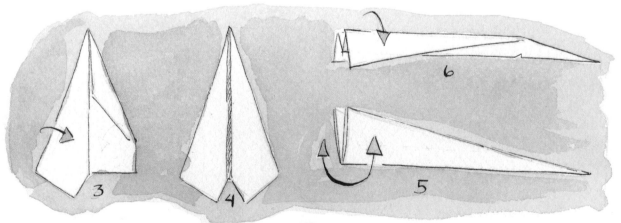

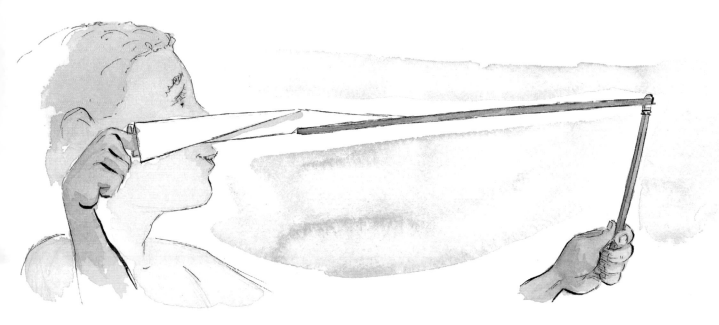

5. Use the yardstick to measure 25 to 40 feet. Mark the start and finish with the tape.

6. Stand at the starting line and launch the plane. Use the stopwatch to time how long it takes the plane to cross the finish line. (A friend may be helpful in this endeavor.)

7. Calculate the speed of the plane by dividing the distance the plane traveled by the amount of time it took.

8. Experiment with making little bends and folds in the wings of your airplane. Can you make your airplane fly faster? Do any of the folds make your airplane fly erratically?

What's Going On?

You have probably seen jets screaming through the air. Their **force** comes from their engines. You supply the force for your jet. The stretched rubber band gives it **energy**, and the jet sails. All planes fly because of **Bernoulli's Principle**. Air rushing over the wing creates **lift** and also gives **stability**. By adjusting the flaps on the wings, you can get your plane to do crazy things.

Pilots adjust the flaps on airplane wings to change the altitude of the plane (make it fly higher or lower) and to steer the plane.

Shark Fins

Control the flight of a rocket with an index card (or two).

What You Need

- Long skinny balloon
- Index cards
- Scissors
- Clothespin or twist tie
- Tape

What You Do

1. Blow up a balloon but do not knot the end. Let the balloon go and watch it zip around.

2. Cut three or four triangles from the index card. Bend a flat area on each triangle so they will stand up on a table. These will be your fins.

3. Blow up the balloon and use the clothespin to hold the nozzle closed. Tape the flat area of a triangle to the nozzle end of the balloon (see illustration). Tape the rest of the fins at equal distances around the balloon. Now unclip the clothespin and let it go. Does the flight pattern change?

4. Try putting small bends on the edges of the fins and see what happens. Experiment with adding a greater or fewer number of fins to the rocket.

What's Going On?

The balloon moves in the exact opposite direction of the nozzle because of **Newton's Third Law** (every **action** has an equal and opposite **reaction**). Since it's made out of rubber, the nozzle can change directions and the balloon flies erratically. The fins create **stability** by directing the **force** of the air. The fins are similar to the keel on a sailboat, the fins on a surfboard, and feathers on an arrow. Fins will help you only in the presence of air, so they're not needed in space, which means space rockets can be any shape.

74

Blast Off!

If your brain is busy working out how and what to catapult next, then your scientific curiosity is soaring sky-high and our work here is done. Thanks for being part of our crashing, smashing, and launching adventures!

If you loved this book, check out *Cool Chemistry Concoctions: 50 Formulas that Fizz, Foam, Splatter & Ooze*, in which we turn Lucinda's garage into a chemistry lab.

You can astound your friends and family with science tricks that work like magic with the help of another one of our books, *It's Not Magic, It's Science!*

And, of course, there's a book for your four (or more) footed friends: *Pet Science: 50 Purr-fectly Woof-Worthy Activities for You & Your Pets.*

Glossary

Acceleration. The rate an object's speed (or direction) changes over a certain period of time

Action. To do something; any use of energy

Aerodynamics. The study of how gases move and how forces and objects move in relation to them

Airfoil. A surface that air flows around, using Bernoulli's Principle to create lift

Air pressure. The pressure exerted on everything on Earth by the weight of air

Arch. A shape comprised of two points connected by a curve that distributes force over a larger area

Area. The amount of space, usually measured on a solid surface or plane

Atom. A tiny unit of matter that makes up a molecule. It contains electrons, neutrons, and protons

Balanced forces. A stable state in which all forces are cancelled by opposing forces

Bernoulli's Principle. When the speed of a fluid (water, air, oil, etc.) increases, its pressure decreases

Buoyant force. An upward force created by the difference in pressure on the top and bottom of an object

Catapult. A device that is pulled back and then let go, launching projectiles using stored energy

Centripetal force. The type of force that pulls an object in a circle around a center point

Chemical reaction. See reaction

Collision. When one object smacks, bumps, or touches another object, resulting in a change of momentum and energy

Conductor. A substance through which electrical charges or heat can easily flow

Conserved energy. The amount of energy stays the same, even when the type of energy changes

Counteract. To oppose a force with an equal, balancing force

Delta wing airfoil. Triangular airfoil. See airfoil

Density. The amount of mass per unit of volume of a substance; its thickness or concentration

Destructology. A subset of physics, invented by Jessie, Lucinda, and Tim, devoted to the study of impact explosions

Elastic collision. A collision between two objects in which the total kinetic energy is conserved, and both objects have the same momentum as before

Elastic materials. Solids that return to their original sizes and shapes after being stretched or compressed

Electric field. An area in which the force of electric charge exists

Electromagnetic wave. Energy waves such as light waves, radio waves, microwaves, and x-rays composed of oscillating electrical and magnetic fields

Electromagnetic radiation. Energy that moves as magnetic waves, as electric waves, and in photons

Electron. A particle of the atom having a negative electrical charge

Energy. The ability to do work, such as applying force or making any object move

Filament. A thin fiber or wire. In a bulb, electrons move through it, creating light

Flap. A flat piece of material attached horizontally, used for directing force up and down

Force. A push or a pull that gives energy to an object

Friction. Resistance between moving objects or a moving object and a stationary object

Gas. A substance, such as air, that is neither a liquid nor a solid and has the ability to expand infinitely

Gravity. The natural force of attraction exerted between two objects that tends to draw them toward the center of the more massive object

Horizontal force. Force applied in the direction parallel to the ground and at right angles to the vertical

Impulse. Force multiplied by time in a collision

Inelastic collision. A collision between two bodies in which the kinetic energy is transformed to another form of energy

Inertia. An object in motion will stay in motion, and an object at rest will stay at rest until acted upon by an outside force

Kinetic energy. The energy a body has because of being in motion, dependent on its speed and mass

Law of Conservation of Energy. Energy can neither be created nor destroyed and always remains a constant amount

Law of Conservation of Momentum. The amount of momentum does not change. For example, in a collision, momentum lost by one object is equal to the momentum gained by the other

Lift. An upward force

Magnus Effect. The perpendicular force that causes a spinning object to curve in its path

Mass. The amount of matter packed into a certain space; its weight

Microwave. A high-frequency radio wave. *See radiowave*

Molecules. The smallest particle of substance, usually composed of two or more atoms

Momentum. The measure of a body's motion; the product of its mass and velocity

Motion. The act or process of changing position or place

Newton's First Law of Motion. A body at rest tends to stay at rest and a body in motion tends to stay in motion unless an outside force acts upon the body. This is the principle that explains inertia

Newton's Second Law of Motion. The acceleration of a body times its mass is equal to the total force acting on the body

Newton's Third Law of Motion. Every action has an opposite and equal reaction

$P=F/A$. The mathematical calculation for pressure, force divided by area

Parabola. A curve formed by points that are the same distance from a line and a given point that is not on that line

Potential energy. The energy a body has because of its position or condition rather than its motion

Pressure. Force applied to or distributed over a surface

Projectile. An object that can be propelled by an outside force acting on it, but cannot move itself

Radio wave. An electromagnetic wave with the lowest frequency and longest wave length used for radio and television broadcasting as well as in microwave ovens

Reaction. A response to an action or substance

Resistance. A force, such as friction, that opposes motion

Rest. The absence of motion; still, quiet, or inactive

Rotational. Moving around a center point

Rudder. A hinged piece of material used for steering airplanes and boats or otherwise directing force

Sound waves. The energy produced by a sound. The energy moves outward as a wave in all directions and is carried by a solid, liquid, or gas

Speed. The rate of motion; distance divided by time

Stability. Balanced, not subject to change

Terminal velocity. The constant rate, determined by an objects' shape and weight, at which air resistance causes falling objects to stop accelerating

Thermal energy. The energy of heat

Time. A measurable sequence in which events happen

Torque. A rotational force

Trajectory. The curved path through space that a projectile forms when it is launched

Trusses. A triangular frame of bars that distribute weight in buildings and bridges

Ultraviolet light. A part of the electromagnetic spectrum with wavelengths longer than x-rays and shorter than visible light

Unbalanced forces. A state in which one force acting on an object is stronger than the other forces acting on that object

Velocity. The speed at which an object moves in a particular direction

Vertical force. Force applied up or down

Visible light. The part of the electromagnetic spectrum, located between ultraviolet light and x-rays, that we can see

Volume. The amount of space taken up by a liquid, solid, or gas

Wedge. An object that is thick on one end and narrows to an edge or point at the other

Weight. The force with which an object is attracted to Earth or another celestial body by gravity, dependent on the object's mass and the strength of gravity's pull

X-ray. High energy electromagnetic radiation with a wavelength shorter than ultraviolet light and longer than a gamma ray

Acknowledgments

Explosions of gratitude to Michele Mercer for her patience and understanding. She always ignores the mess in the kitchen and lets Bobby use the microwave for science experiments. Thank you also to Nicole, for occasionally remaining at rest so that her daddy could stay in motion and at work on his manuscript.

Thanks to everybody in the Children's Department at Lark Books, especially to Rose McLarney, Celia Naranjo, and Bradley Norris. They really made this book blast off!

The assistance of Sherry Hames and Chris Clarke was as invaluable and dependable as Newton's Laws. They improved the clarity of the explanations.

Thanks to Tom LaBaff and his children, who enthusiastically tested many of the experiments in this book so that their dad could draw them perfectly.

Metric Conversions

To convert degrees Fahrenheit to degrees Celsius, subtract 32 and then multiply by .56.
To convert inches to centimeters, multiply by 2.5.
To convert ounces to grams, multiply by 28.
To convert teaspoons to milliliters, multiply by 5.
To convert tablespoons to milliliters, multiply by 15.
To convert fluid ounces to milliliters, multiply by 30.
To convert cups to liters, multiply by .24.

Index